A Patriots Voice

(Under Democrat Rule)

Anna Harris

Balboa Press books may be ordered through booksellers or by contacting:

Balboa Press
A Division of Hay House
1663 Liberty Drive
Bloomington, IN 47403
www.balboapress.com
844-682-1282

ISBN: 979-8-7652-2506-6 (sc)
ISBN: 979-8-7652-2507-3 (e)

Print information available on the last page.

Balboa Press rev. date: 02/22/2022

BALBOA.PRESS
A DIVISION OF HAY HOUSE

To My Family,
Service Members,
and First Responders.

Thank You!
God Bless You!
And God Bless America!

A Patriots Voice

(Under Democrat Rule)

Table of Contents

My pen is my voice.. 1

Red & Blue 21 2

Sold Out 5

Their Mission: Fear 7

Silenced 9

Let Us Stay 11

The Children 13

A Passing Dream 15

Just 2 Weeks 17

Just Smile 19

Help Us God 21

Still Free 23

Day Dreaming 25

Quiet 27

Education... 29

No Border Wall...31

A Conservative Shout 33

Left Behind 35

Bad Mistake 37

What's Going on in this World 39

My pen is my voice

I keep it near crying inside
to mask my fear

Red & Blue 21

(bound & gagged)

I am bleeding blue cause the wounds are within
So worried for myself & my kin

The boarder is crawling with despair
and distress "Come on man what a mess"

I look to my left
I look to my right, but there's no help in sight
(Lay down can't even sleep at night)

I would jump in my car to take a
spin, but fraid of blow'n to much carb'n

They're coming for this
They're coming for that so sorry cat in the hat.

Don't worry its not only you
heard them mention speedy a time or two

This isn't cool this isn't fun
now they say they're coming for my gun!

You ask why, but I don't dare start to
think they just don't care

They cry race race
as they spit in our face

We all know this isn't the case

This is a big power grab they
know what they're doing as they
slowly bring our country to ruin

Now the tide has turned the blood
is red can't seen to shake these
thoughts from my head

I'll go to sleep then I'll awake
just to see the news is still fake

As I start my day I pace the floor
only dreaming of "24"

I sit here bound & gagged with no voice
praying to God we still have a choice
Hoping its not too late when you
realize its true, today its me,
tomorrow could be you

I heard it said united we stand
divided we fall

Let this be a lesson to us all

Sold Out

I want to cry
I want to pout
Can't believe you sold us out
I want to scream
I want to ball
Why won't you let them finish the wall

This invasion is never ending and
all you do is increase our spending

You've cut off our feet
Left us to bleed in the street
Oh how I long for your defeat

As I look up I still see light
letting me know I am still in this fight

I'll hold my head up strong and proud

Praying to God and screaming out loud
to all you patriots that feel my pain
lets stick together as they go insane

Knowing we're in it for love
They're in it for gain

This will soon be over just one more campaign

Their Mission: Fear

We will not be ruled by fear
though it seems their mission is clear

This plight we find ourselves in is
driven by evil & sin

We look to the heavens for
strength and endurance

Hoping for change and God's reassurance

Together we stand in this difficult time
as the world watches America unwind

Stoked by hate
Fueled by fear
Feeling like the end is near

We will stand strong and weather this
storm saluting old glory
though tattered and torn

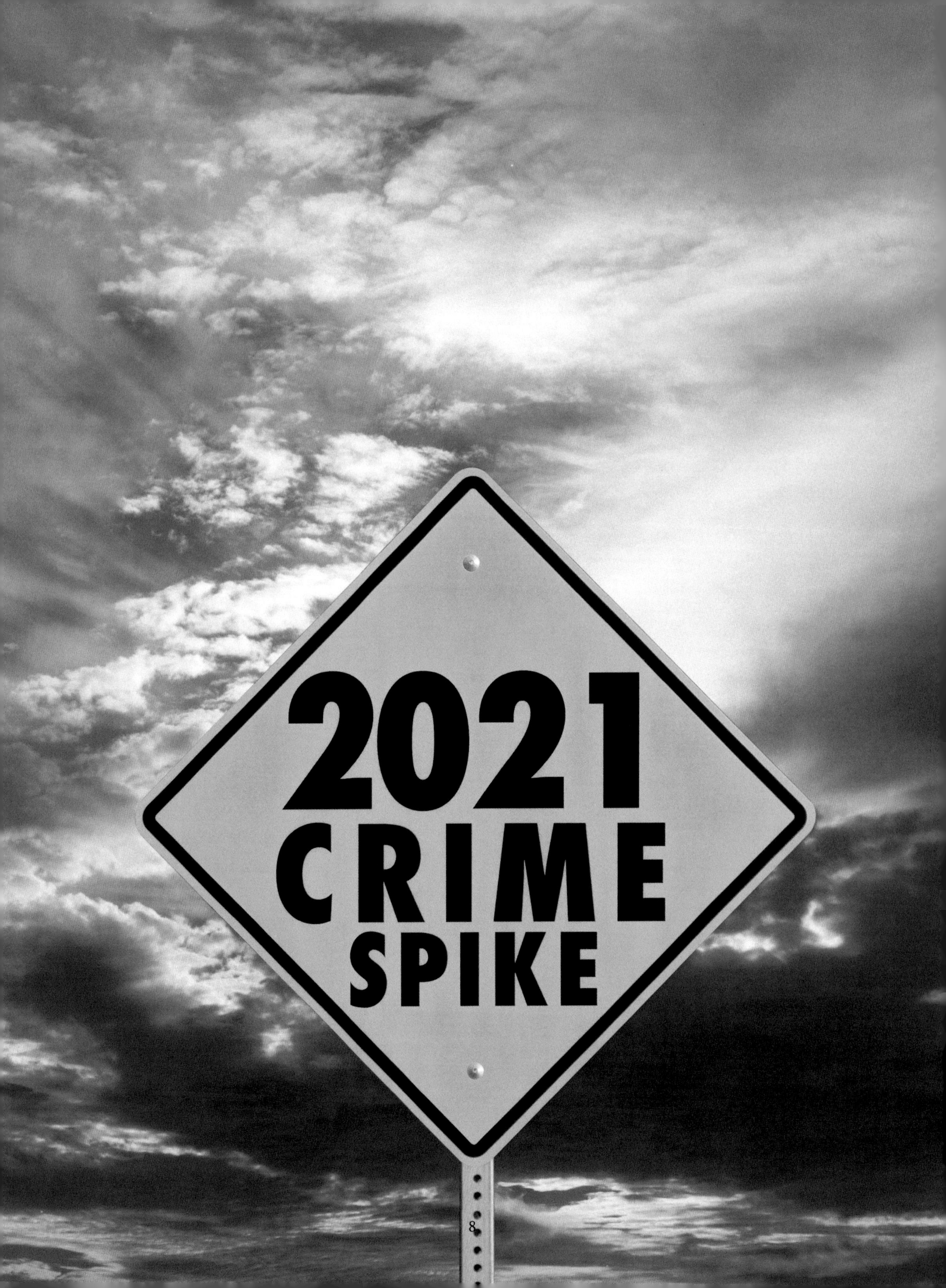
2021
CRIME
SPIKE

Silenced

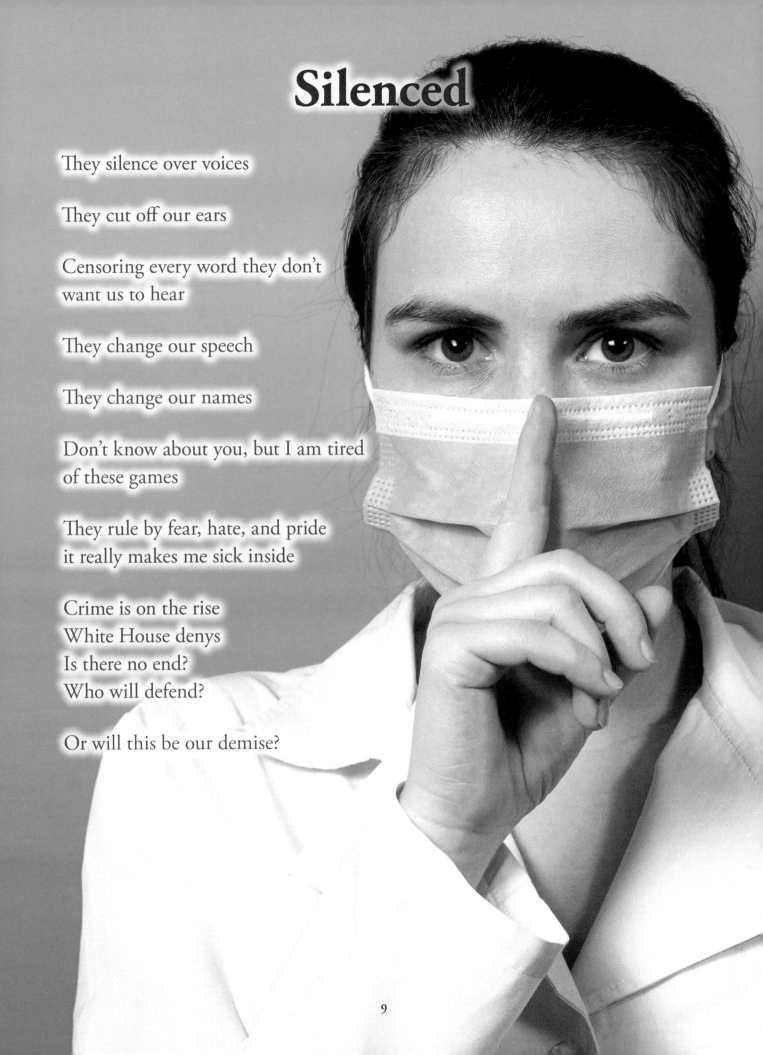

They silence over voices

They cut off our ears

Censoring every word they don't
want us to hear

They change our speech

They change our names

Don't know about you, but I am tired
of these games

They rule by fear, hate, and pride
it really makes me sick inside

Crime is on the rise
White House denys
Is there no end?
Who will defend?

Or will this be our demise?

Let Us Stay

They tell us this
They tell us that

They change their minds
They're soft on crime
Now they want us to drop a dime

They make the rules that they break
They call us fools
They're so fake

Don't know how this all will end, but as
for me and mine we will defend our
countries flag, that flies high and free,
no wonder so many flee, to this land so
far away praying to God just let us stay

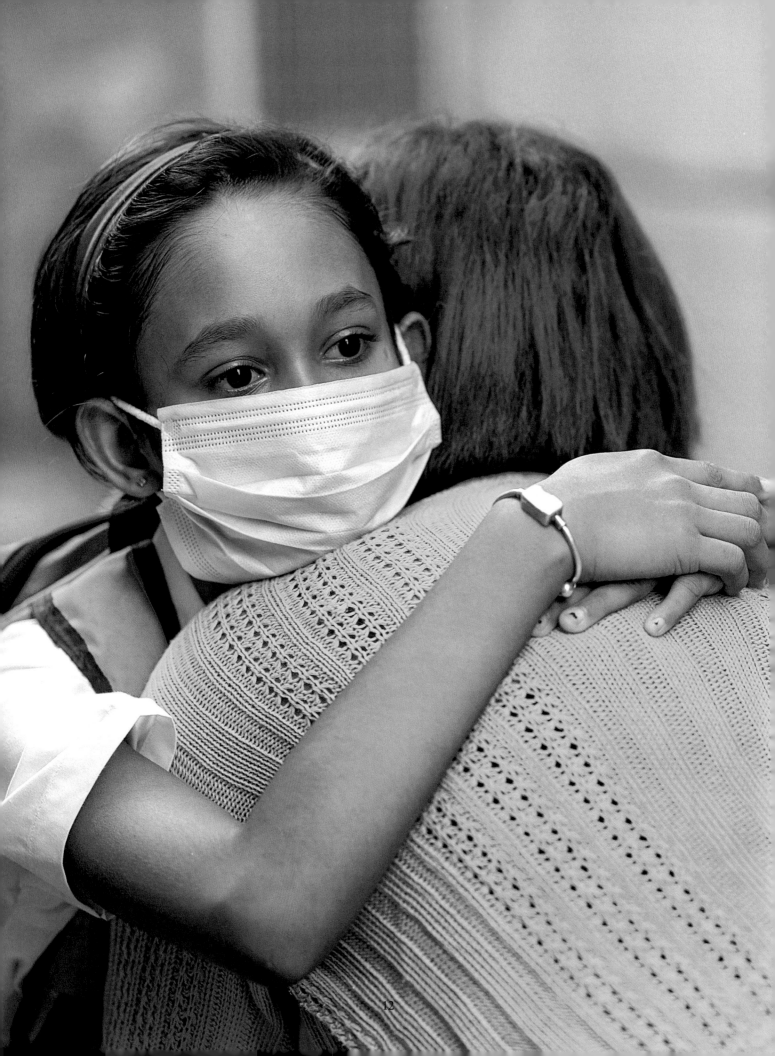

The Children

So innocent and small
Should we even wear masks at all?

Why would they do this?
Does anyone care?

If you open the schools I'll see you there

I want to learn about the past
with math and science in a small class

Is this really too much to ask?

It all seems so silly I must say
I just want to learn, run, and play

Will you allow me this time with my friends
or is it all politics?
I guess that depends

Who will win the left or the right?
I really shouldn't be in this fight

I like the way it was
so please figure this out
cause my stomach hurts
and I want to go out

A Passing Dream

I used to dream I sat by
a brook, with a phone in my
hand and a fish on my hook
now its a mask on my face
and a tear in my eye waiting
and watching the world go by

Just 2 Weeks

Just two weeks I heard them say
then your children can run and play

Just two weeks I thought they said
close your doors to slow the spread

Just two weeks not much more and
wear your masks to the store

Just two weeks with masks and social
distance don't you dare show resistance

Just two weeks now don't you fret
a day is coming we'll all regret

Just two weeks plus a year
did you think we'd still be here?

18

Just Smile

I miss your whole face
though your eyes sparkle and shine

I just need to see you smile
sometime

To see your lip quiver when you shiver
or your quirky grin above your chin
or to blow a kiss

That's what I miss

Help Us God

We are headed for a fall
we cannot break if we make
this fatal mistake

Forgetting the word that's fast and true

Oh help us God
save our red white and blue

Still Free

The sky is blue
The blood is red
have you not heard a word I said

The fight is real its here and now
so take off your mask and take a bow

We are free no matter what they say
to solute our flag and thank God for
each and every day

Day Dreaming

I sit here staring at the clouds
wondering what I could do
to unsilence the crowd

We need to wake up now more
than ever cause they're shrewd,
unkind, and clever

Make no mistake they're playing
for keeps as they riot, kill, and vandalize
our streets

We need to take a firm stance now
Not tomorrow!
For if we don't, all that's ahead
is hurt, pain, and sorrow

Quiet

Don't ask questions
Do as I say
No you can't go out and play
There is crime in the street
Blood at our feet
So much anger, hate, and deceit

Education

Education is drowning
I hear that sound

Come on people! "look around"

Can't you see these kids are yerning
so sick and tired of online learning

No Border Wall

"Don't come," I didn't hear her say
so hurry up family don't delay
to the land of the free
"Well at least for me"
"Come one, Come all"

Hop, skip, or crawl
for you see there is no border wall!

A Conservative Shout

A conservative shout

Let's get them out!!

With all your sin you cannot win

Our children's dreams hang in the balance

To all your socialist we don't need your allowance

You rant and you rave, but we will not cave

With our voices like thunder we will watch you go under and in all your discrace
we will win this next race

Left Behind

As evil looms across the globe
I really fear my heart could explode

I watch helplessly as mothers plead
for help that they and their children
so desperately need

They are under attack its very clear,
but all their screaming falls on a deaf ear

We fought side by side
how could we be so blind, but as the
planes take off, to the skies they
climb looking up realizing we're left behind

Bad Mistake

Here is some news that isn't fake

13 service members killed due to your mistake

Blood on the streets
Blood on your hands

No one is happy not even your fans

You better step up and do the right thing cause God only knows the hell it will bring

What's Going on in this World

What's going on in this world
Boys are girls
Girls are boys

Don't even think about Christmas toys
"Let's go Brandon!"

Our shelves are bare
There's no planes in the air
Ships are docked at the ports
Containers everywhere
"Let's go Brandon!"

Our children are targets of this admin.
While we're supposed to take it on the chin

Gas prices soar
There's no food in the store
"Let's go Brandon!"

While I sit here in amazement wondering
what to do, who to blame, I truly know
we can not endure more of the same
So get out and vote don't make it a chore
cause fast approaching is "2024"
"Let's go Brandon!"

Printed in the United States
by Baker & Taylor Publisher Services